Buffets

A GUIDE FOR PROFESSIONALS

Buffets

A GUIDE ❧
FOR PROFESSIONALS

Georges C. St. Laurent, Jr.
Chet Holden

JOHN WILEY & SONS

New York   Chichester   Brisbane   Toronto   Singapore

Cover photo: Riccardo Marcialis
Production supervisor: Fred Schulte
Interior design: Laura Ierardi/Dawn L. Stanley
Cover design: Dawn L. Stanley

Library of Congress Cataloging in Publication Data

St. Laurent, Jr., Georges C.
Buffets: a guide for professionals.

Bibliography: p.
Includes index.
    1. Buffets (Cookery)   2. Quantity cookery.
I. Holden, Chet. II. Title.
TX738.5.S73 1986   642'.4   85-22677
ISBN 0-471-83229-4

Printed in the United States of America

10 9 8 7

Printed and bound by the Arcata Graphics Company.

Dedication

The authors respectfully dedicate BUFFETS to Mrs. Eleanor "Toodie" St. Laurent, and her sons Georges III and William.

Preface

In his delightful book *Ma Gastronomie*, the late French master chef Fernand Point reflected: "If the divine creator has taken pains to give us delicious and exquisite things to eat, the least we can do is prepare them well and serve them with ceremony." Nowhere is this more true than in the vast and wonderful realm of buffets.

Every time we set up banquet tables, drape them with crisp linen, and polish the chafers, we present a food-service format that enables us to transcend the cuisine of this nation and all others. All countries or cooking styles are represented in this culinary bandwagon, as are all segments of the American food-service industry. From morning to midnight, juice bar to happy hour, Sunday brunch to Monday night football . . . the sun never sets on the world of buffets.

The treatment of so vast a subject is a challenge. The question is not so much where to begin but, rather, where to end. What we have done with Buffets is to offer bits and pieces, a taste of this and a sample of that, in much the same way our subject itself comes to life on food-service tables. Each subject will be "garnished" in a different way, as if the very world of cooking might join our food parade. It is our intention that each chapter should stand as a building block of information, firm in its own content yet stronger when combined with the material from others.

A GLOBAL PERSPECTIVE. Yes, there is indeed a world of buffets. We offer a guide to a score of countries, their foods, and their customs. From within the quiet valleys of a far-off land come ideas that can take their place on your buffet tables. Come one, come all to this wonderful world of foods!

HERBS AND SPICES. If there is a key to unlocking the treasures of ethnic cookery, surely it will be found within the array of herbs and spices that have traveled from around the globe to lend airs to our own kitchens. We will review dozens of these seeds, nuts, and leaves and offer you some suggestions for how best to use each of them.

APPETIZERS. Buffet favorites throughout the culinary universe, in some cultures appetizers actually represent the entire buffet array. We will look at some of these appetizer settings and suggest ways of incorporating them in your buffet presentations.

SALADS.   Salad ingredients are listed on market sheets throughout the year, but at some times the quality and economy of fruits and vegetables definitely encourage their use in meal planning. We will look at the seasons for our nation's vitamin-rich harvest.

SOUPS.   Soups appear on more international menus than perhaps any other course, and every country has a few that stand as national favorites. We will highlight a soup from each of almost 50 countries and domestic recipes as well — every one a proven success.

MEATS.   Viewed in terms of their place in global cookery, meats are discussed in a way that includes a taste of Greek lamb, Chinese pork, British beef, German sausage . . . and more.

SEAFOOD.   Considering the multitude of species available, seafood can be a real mystery in food planning. But in Chapter 7 you will learn to separate varieties into interchangeable and, therefore, highly usable lean/fat categories.

POULTRY.   Every nation of this world cooks and serves poultry, be it duck or quail, chicken or goose, turkey or Cornish hen. We will take a country-by-country look at some long-standing multinational favorites.

SIDE DISHES.   Vegetables will be presented by their country of origin, so you can learn in just which cooking styles they naturally appear. Are potatoes appropriate in the Orient, or might they best be served on a Brazilian buffet?

DESSERTS.   Creativity in desserts is of paramount concern for buffet planners who must continually find new dishes to tempt and tantalize. Buffets offers a profile of dessert classics to help keep the meal's end at the top of any menu's excitement.

BRUNCH.   This is a profitable meal for food-service buffets, and one that often focuses on eggs. We will borrow from some French classics to suggest a hundred ways in which to cook these brunchtime specialties.

Our "buffet" will offer an array of tastes and textures, a panorama of color and cooking. We hope that your moments of reading and the menus you plan will be influenced by the subjects we have chosen. But more than that, if we encourage you to continue the search for another buffet theme, another dish to add to your menu repertoire, then our efforts will have been successful.

CARE, the worldwide food relief agency, once circulated a simple wall poster that stated: "If you give a man a fish, you feed him for a day. If you teach a man to fish, you feed him for his lifetime." We sincerely hope that Buffets will teach you something lasting about a truly universal style of service.

GEORGES C. ST. LAURENT, JR.
CHET HOLDEN

About
the Recipes

You will find more than 300 recipes in the pages that follow. We have attempted to provide a broad cross section of ethnic as well as regional American foods so that you can add to your existing buffet menus or perhaps gain insight into new themes for service.

It was not our goal to dictate complete buffet menus but to spark interest in the subject and to prompt additional research.

Every recipe includes quantities for testing as well as for service.

In a buffet environment, it is difficult to establish exact portion quantities because guests are invited to help themselves. However, we have suggested 8 portions for the test quantity and 50 for service. Your experience will allow you to fine-tune these quantities through repeated use.

We have also included suggestions for proper service of each dish and some hints on variations. Garnishing ideas will be discussed in the chapter on buffet layout. We hope that the remaining text material will help you to supplement each recipe with seasonings and ingredients that are appropriate for each dish. Through experimentation in cooking and service, the world of buffets can become a profitable part of your menu repertoire.

Table of Contents

Acknowledgments

We are grateful for the assistance of several good friends and colleagues, whose kind words and deeds had great impact on the content of the following pages. We thank them with sincerity and respect.

Brother Herman E. Zaccarelli—Director of Purdue University's Restaurant, Hotel and Institutional Management Institute.

Ferdinand E. Metz—President, The Culinary Institute of America, Hyde Park, New York.

The International Foodservice Editorial Council—Several of whose members donated time, recipes and the beautiful photographic plates that grace several pages within the book.

The Professional Review Committee—Several professionals from the field of foodservice who spend many hours reading, reviewing and—thankfully—correcting manuscript.

Judith Joseph—Editor, John Wiley and Sons, Inc. who supported the project with enthusiasm and constructive support, literally from its very genesis.

We also acknowledge the following individuals for their contributions: John R. McDonald, The Southeast Institute of Culinary Arts/St. Augustine Technical Center; Patrick Sweeney, Johnson County Community College; Mike Jung, Hennepin Technical Centers; Valeria S. Mason, State Department of Education, Gainesville, Florida; Philip Panzarino, New York City Community College; Herb Traub, Pirates' House, Savannah, Georgia; Gayle M. Müller, Keystone Junior College; and George Dragisity, University of Houston.

G. C. ST. L., Jr.
C. H.

One

Buffets: A Global Perspective

The development of any national cuisine is a function of various factors. Just as climate and geography are surely influential, so too are social and religious customs. Around the world, when people gather to observe and celebrate traditional occasions, very often the focal point is food. Great buffet tables are laden with fare of all descriptions. So let's look at some international themes that you might consider adding to your list of buffet possibilities.

Austria. Austrian cooking (often called Viennese) is one of the world's more heterogeneous culinary styles, reflecting influences of Italy, Hungary, Poland, Rumania, France, and Germany. This mixed-bag cuisine presents Viennese fried chicken beside boiled beef with chives, apple sauce with horseradish, and slices of Sacher torte. Pastries are legion, and when it comes to buffets, Austrians gather in hordes. Whether it's the chic Viennese Opera Ball, a candlelit New Year's Eve, or a pre–Lenten herring feast, Austrians revel in buffets. All of Austria's culinary festivities offer suggestions for American menu writing; check your calendar, as the Austrians do, for "pudding week," "dumpling week," or "game week."

Czechoslovakia. A blend of Eastern European foods join German and Austrian influences in the Bohemian style of

Czechoslovakia. Smoked Prague ham is famous, as are buffets that celebrate the use of pork. Lard is the choice over butter, and sausages are national favorites. Sour cream and sauerkraut, pickles and dumplings are Czech favorites. Fish (be it trout or prized carp) are often the centerpiece for Christmas buffets, while broiled lamb, gnocchi, pickled vegetables, and a variety of bread are highlights of the nationally popular Czech fishing picnics. If you want to duplicate a Czech fishing festival, set the table in green linen and drape it with netting; be sure to have beer and Riesling wine to accompany the meal. Traditional with Czech men is a stag party in honor of someone's fiftieth birthday; hunt festivals in the fall honor the tradition of setting all glasses to the left (leaving room on the right for weapons) and the use of round tables to assure equal status for all.

Denmark. The most famous Danish buffet is a culinary art form in its own right: The *smørrebrød* (translating simply to "bread and butter") is a buffet of open-faced sandwiches with literally hundreds of variations. Resting atop thin slices of diverse breads are profuse combinations of eggs, radishes, pickles, sardines, anchovies, lettuces, pickles, shrimp, onions, cheese, sour cream, capers, potatoes, and caviar . . . and that is just the tip of a very tasty Danish culinary iceberg. But buffets are not limited to the *smørrebrød* in this country known for

hams and bacon. On Christmas Eve there is a grand feast with pork, goose, goose, traditional rice dishes, and apple cake with cream; Christmas Day is characterized by much simpler fare, with liver pâtés and bread. Breakfast pastries known throughout the world as "Danish" are here called "Vienna breads" and are popular on the breakfast bar with juices, butter, and jams. Danes serve boiled cod at the New Year's Eve fête and always offer aquavit to drink. Traditional buffets also include the Round Year party, a celebration held every decade from an individual's tenth birthday to the one-hundredth and beyond; fruited cakes are bedecked with whipped cream for these occasions.

Finland. Rains fall frequently in this Scandinavian land, all the better for her wondrous wild mushrooms and ever-popular potatoes; it is said that the latter rival any spud on earth. The sea offers Finns a bounty of species, including the favored herring. Buffet season is an all-year affair, with high points that include the Christian holidays of Easter, Advent, and Christmas. A customary dish on the yuletide buffet is almond rice, a seasonal specialty in which nestles a hidden nut, awaiting the first single person to find it and "assuring" marriage within the year. May Day is a secular observance, as the coming spring is a welcomed break from the long and trying winter months. The May Day buffet is actually a breakfast that follows a full night of revelry; herring, in many styles, steals the show and is complemented with breads, golden butter, and the omnipresent schnapps and beer. Once the summer has fully unfolded, Finns celebrate Midsummer's Eve, a bonfire-torched affair that features, among other favorites, Russian-influenced blinis and vodka.

France. What has yet to be said about the cuisine of France? Perhaps only China can compete with this European nation when it comes to an influence on global cooking. To look at France is to look at a country of regions, each brimming with opportunity for buffet themes. Take Normandy, for example. Offer guests poached fish with sorrel or sautéed veal with mushrooms and apples. From the Alsace region, offer pork in almost any form (it's the region's favorite meat) or spark up some pheasant with sausages and sauerkraut for a variation on the *choucroute* theme. The Burgundy region brings great wines put to wonderful use in the classic chicken dish known as *coq au vin.* Another Burgundian delight is *gougère,* a feather-light pastry made to nibble with wine; with or without a sauce to accompany, this cheesey, choux-based pastry will enliven your buffet. The Lyonnaise region, known for its great restaurants, is also famous for its cheeses. Offer a selection of cheeses and a brioche dough with sausage (*saucisson en brioche*) and glasses of wine for a buffet delight. For a taste of Provence, intermingle slices of tomato and zucchini in a steam table pan; top with sautéed garlic, onions, eggplant, and peppers; drizzle with olive oil and bake.

Great Britain. Long the subject of snide culinary references, British cuisine in fact offers wonderful meats and game to accompany her abundant fruits and rich Cheddar and Stilton cheeses. Buffets range from a high tea and formal wedding luncheon to perhaps the grandest British meal, breakfast. Porridge and other cereals, fruits, bacon, ham, sausage, eggs, breads, and traditional finnan haddie are offered daily; on special occasions, like a hunt breakfast, there are hors d'oeuvres, cold meats, and more hot fish to bolster the buffet. Sporting people to the end, Britons take special pains at buffets that celebrate the Henley Regatta in June (strawberries and thick Devonshire cream) or Derby Day at Epsom Downs; cold meats (pâtés, gallantines, terrines) or fish (poached lobster or salmon) will receive special buffet treatment. And no summer is complete without the Ascot races and their parades of food and drink, pomp and circumstance. At yuletide, the turkey displaces the regal goose on many buffet tables, but flaming plum pudding remains a tradition. In fact, puddings of many kinds are often featured in British cuisine.

India. The foods of this country reflect very clearly the influences of religion and geography, as both Hindus (who are vegetarian) and Moslems (who are not) populate this vast nation. Whether the buffet is free of meat according to Hindu tenet or replete with lamb and chicken (especially flavorful is kiln-roasted henna-red "tandoori-style"), Indian food is spirited and colorful. The most famous spread is curry. Custom calls for guests to be offered trays with five small bowls (a buffet already!); patna (medium-grain) rice fills one, while chutney, pickled vege- tables, coconut, and *pappadums* (spicy pepper wafers) are offered in the others. Indian curry is not the prepared powder commonly available here but, rather, a mixture of herbs and spices ground daily to a paste for specific foods. Other items on an Indian buffet may include *sambals* (Indian appetizers), *chapattis* (flat breads), and *samosas* (fried puffs filled with many wonders.) Translated loosely as "pepper water," *mulligatawny* is a fiesty Southern Indian soup that has enjoyed Western popularity. In any Indian buffet, sweets (called *meetais*) are absolutely necessary; essential to every meal, meetais are often brought to a party by guests, who have made them at home. Also critical to most Indian food is *garam masala,* a spice blend that varies from one cook (or food) to another. Variations abound, but garam masala is always ground fresh.

Italy. The first European cookbook ever published emanated from Italy 18 years before Columbus set sail for the New World; to this day Italian cuisine enjoys enormous popularity. Just about any occasion is celebrated with buffet assortments, be it a New Year's Day lentil dish ("lots of lentils bring lots of money") or a predinner antipasto selection of meats, cheeses, artichokes, and olives. The predominantly Roman Catholic population has established a number of church-related holidays that lend themselves naturally to food. Epiphany (in English, the Twelfth Night) is January 6; Carnival (Shrovetide) is a time for fritters and lasagna, especially in Naples. Easter is a day for lamb, and the following day, Easter Monday, is traditional as the *pic-nic de Pasquetta* or the first picnic of the new spring; roast chicken and frittata slices are served with cheeses and jugs of wine. All Hallows is a family time where pastries and marzipan figures that represent famous characters are served. On Martinmas (November 11), chestnuts are served (traditionally alongside a bonfire) with wine. For Christmas Eve, there is a vast seafood buffet; the chafers of this peninsular nation are filled with squid, octopus, clams, mussels, and fish of all descriptions.

Japan. The culinary displays of this nation bring buffets to magnificent heights. Japanese chefs are masters of the knife, and when these talents are applied to ice carvings, the effects are dramatic. Sushi and sashimi arrangements take on mosaic charms; and then there are the *bento,* literally "picnic box," foods. *Yakitori* are grilled chicken strips served on a skewer with soy sauce, tempura are batter-fried meats and vegetables served with dipping condiments, and *onigariyaki* is a seafood kebab with shrimp or mussels; each can be prepared by cooks behind the buffet line for guests as they pass by. Soup is served at every Japanese buffet, be it *akadashi* at breakfast (a red miso soup often served with tofu), *sumashijiru* at lunch (a clear chicken soup), or *hamaguri no ushio jiru* at dinner (a clam consommé). Pickled vegetables are also popular, as are many kinds of fish; remember, Japan is comprised of a chain of islands. Steamed rice (*gohan*) is a Japanese standard. Most Japanese buffets end rather simply, with freshly cut fruits arranged artistically. Garnishes of serrated palm leaves and small bowls of piquant green horseradish (*wasabo*) help to decorate the Japanese buffet table.

Mexico. One of the food industry's most popular ethnic trends, Mexican cookery has withstood the test of time. With a blend of Indian and Spanish touches, Mexican food can form a central theme for your buffet schedules—and it's not all tacos and beans. Take the piñata party. The celebration of a birthday can prompt the breaking of a piñata stuffed with candies, balloons, and other treats. Or feature an afternoon *merienda,* a Mexican variation of the British tea party. Coffee is the choice now, though, accompanied with pastries and Mexican coffee—equal parts of steaming brew and hot milk. Two festive occasions to celebrate with a Mexican flare are January 6, the traditional Twelfth Night, and May 5, *El Cinco de Mayo,* the Mexican day of Independence. Don't stick to the Tex-Mex favorites, but venture instead into the Yucatán for lime soup or garlic-laced pompano fillets. Look to the hill country for the Mexican standard, *mole poblano;* use chicken or turkey as you wish. One can also savor the southern coast of Mexico by offering *camarones en frio,* which are cold marinated prawns lusty with cilantro, garlic, and lime.

The Netherlands. Dutch cuisine reflects not only the bounty of that country's fields and canals, but also the heritage of courageous sailors who unlocked the treasures of exotic Spice Islands. Indonesia, first settled by the Dutch, has contributed the now-famed *rijsttafel* (rice table) to our journey through buffets. Rice holds center stage (literally) but the supporting cast includes a panoply of zesty dishes: fruits, meats, vegetables and fish are served in tidbit portions, made fiery hot with pungent sauces. Be sure to offer cooling tumblers of chilled beer or tea; remember, too, that the rijsttafel tradition excludes the use of knives in favor of forks and spoons. On the holiday side, the Dutch celebrate New Year's Eve in the home of friends, starting with coffee before proceeding through wines and stout Dutch Genever gin; herring is exceedingly popular, as are veal, pork, and chicken. Appetizers on a Dutch buffet will employ shrimp, eel, and oysters that are smoked, salted, marinated, in dill sauce, with tomatoes, and even raw. If early December is in need of an event, follow the Dutch lead with a St. Nicholas Day affair; every December 5, the Dutch celebrate with a grand buffet and then conclude with the tradition of offering all guests their own initials, struck from pure chocolate.

Norway. A land of crystal waters and scarlet cranberries, Norway offers countless variations on the buffet theme. Its fjords yield crayfish; its seashore offers lobster and cod; and its fields offer a great variety of fruits and vegetables. Lamb is prevalent for entrees, beef is stewed with beer and cabbage, and rice desserts are favorites. After the long winter, Norwegians gather to celebrate their national day on May 17; this is the time to flaunt great salmon with hollandaise sauce and cucumbers and strawberries and cream to end. Later in the summer come Midsummer Eve (June 24) and Olsok Day (July 29)—both occasions for grilled or thinly sliced dried lamb. August 8 brings the opening of crayfish season, and in September lobsters make their debut, accompanied by mounds of toast and rich mayonnaise; game begins to appear at this time too. The yuletime *Julebord* is a festive occasion that runs for weeks (December 5 through 20) and is characterized by vast buffets of hot and cold foods. New Year's Eve in Norway is another dining occasion, featuring traditional Norwegian breads (flat, square, thin, thick, black, white) with butters and some favorite cheeses.

Spain. The cookery of Spain reflects its turbulent past. The Romans invaded and brought olive oil. The Moors invaded and brought saffron and rice, without either of which *paella* could not exist. Then when the Spanish set out to do some conquering on their own, they counted among their booty the potato, the tomato, the pepper, and chocolate. The most prolific display of these and other foods is the *tapas* buffet (see Appetizers), a wondrous assortment of tidbits enjoyed with sangria or sherry before a later-evening meal. Andalusia, home of flamenco dancing, is a southern region whose shores produce legions of seafood varieties. This is also the home of another American favorite, gazpacho. The Basque region of Spain celebrates its shepherds with a number of lamb dishes, many of which are served with potatoes. Where the sea meets the herds, a result is salt cod and tomatoes, bean dishes, and famous *chorizos* (sausages). If you wish to put a touch of Catalonia on your buffet table, get out the red pepper and wine; this Spanish district is famous for its feisty sauces. Valencia is the home of a buffet-in-a-pan, the famous paella. Combining the best of sea, shore, and field, paella offers anyone the chance to prepare a buffet with true Old World charm.

Sweden. From the land of the *smörgåsbord* come a number of reasons to gather around the buffet table. Whether it

is Easter (complete with blue and yellow eggs and multicolored feathers) or Midsummer's Eve (with seemingly omnipresent salmon and remoulade sauce), the Swedish are big on buffets. A "morning after the night before" tradition in Sweden is the Vikings table, with herring dishes at its center; salmon, hash, sausages, and cheese are washed down with coffee and glasses of aquavit. But it is the smörgåsbord that puts Sweden on the global buffet map. Not one table, but many, are needed. The first, smallest, table offers breads and cheeses, assorted herring again, and boiled potatoes. Then a larger table offers forms of salmon, prawns, sausages, pâtés, roasts, ribs, chicken, lamb, and ham and salad. Still another table might feature wild mushrooms, omelets, ragouts, and vegetables. Also important to a smörgåsbord is the small cocktail table at the front of the room with beers and aquavit. Just as important is the dessert collection of fruits and cheeses and Swedish black bread.

Switzerland. This country of 22 provinces (or cantons) offers at least that many specialties for buffets. Whether it's regional wines and fruits toward the Italian border, nuts and desserts of the high valleys, or the most common Swiss treat of all, cheese, Switzerland is a harvest basket of foods. A variation on the time-honored Swiss fondue is the raclette of the Valais district. Guests at a buffet queue up for oozy slices of warmed cheese that are scraped off a large chunk and served with bread, salad, and wine. Other folks might be drawn to crudités, a favorite offering of raw vegetables and dips. The Harvest Festival of the Bernese Emmenthal (same name as the famed large-holed cheese) features great sheets of plaited breads, a

traditional pork and veal stew, and the celebrated *Berner platte:* grand sausages and beans or sauerkraut. Desserts might be meringues with whipped cream and coffee laced with cherry kirsch. The canton Fribourg celebrates the *Benichon*, a tribute to fruits and the earth. Breads again are featured, as are soups with vegetables and marrow bones. A special mustard (with the same name as that of the region) is offered with spiced pears and cooked wine; the roasted leg of lamb is served with carmelized apples and pears and the region's grapes. As always, cheeses and eau-de-vie, a clear brandy, end the buffet affair.

Tunisia. Like paella and bouillabaisse, Tunisia's *couscous* is a spicy, one-bowl, full-meal buffet combination of grain (usually semolina) steamed over pots of lamb, chicken, and vegetables; pork is never served. Slices of melon offer a refreshing counterpoint for the feisty tomato-laced sauce. A holiday celebrated by this Islamic nation is Prophet's Day (or *Mouled*), which offers the opportunity to present a great Tunisian favorite, *assida.* This is a sweet served with pastry cream and fruits and is shared throughout the land. Date and walnut cakes are also popular. Fruits are a big part of Tunisian cookery, as are hors d'oeuvres. Not served to begin a meal but throughout, appetizers can take many forms. Fish is popular along the coastline, where it is served as part of the traditional wedding feast. In fact, a fish is placed at the doorstep of the new couple so, as they step over it the day after their betrothal, they will be blessed with good health and a protected home. Although wine is not generally imbibed in Tunisia, a good rosé would complement a regional buffet.

Two

Herbs and Spices; The Bark is the Bite

Herbs and spices, which have been sought throughout history for their pre-serving and flavor-enhancing qualities, can help you to duplicate dishes that their use over time has created. Stored air-tight, cool and dry, and ground a bit before each use, herbs and spices stand ready to guide you through the wonders of multiethnic cuisines.

HERBS

Basil. The French often call basil the "royal herb" in recognition of its culinary diversity; in Greek, the word means "king." The clove/pepper aroma and taste of basil is a natural with lemon and garlic and balances well with mint; a na-tive of India, it has traveled throughout all of Europe and into such New World cook-ing styles as that of Chile. A classic with tomatoes, try basil with corn, zucchini, peas, and eggplant; seafood, sausages, lamb chops, and eggs will also benefit. Fresh cucumber salad with basil, mint, and yogurt will showcase its Mediterra-nean heritage.

Bay Leaf. A primary bouquet garni herb, one well at home in hearty stews, this Middle Eastern herb was used in an-tiquity to honor kings and victors; classic in the French cuisine, a variety of this aromatic plant is now cultivated in Cali-fornia. Best used while green, not dry and brittle, bay leaves should always be added in moderation and removed before service. Pickling brines and marinades often call for bay leaves, as do poaching liquids for poultry and seafood. Cabbage soup, chowders, curries, rice dishes, and stuffings, along with roasted poultry and lamb, are just a few of its many uses.

Caraway. Available in leaf and seed form, this versatile herb has been in use since 5000 B.C.; once thought to settle stomachs, it has become a major culinary ingredient in several cuisines. Offering a taste profile of dill and anise, caraway shows up in Scandinavian, Polish, and Hungarian dishes as well as in the cordial Kummel; it is a major flavoring in rye bread. Try adding caraway seeds to sau-erkraut and cabbage, baked apples, po-tato salad, cakes, carrots, beets, noodles, and goulash; the leaves are ideal for stews, meat loaf, green salad, and egg-plant.

Chervil. Native to southwest Asia, chervil contributes a light anise flavor to fish and chicken dishes, omelets, soups, and sauces. A relative of the carrot fam-ily, chervil is combined with tarragon, chives, and parsley to form the French blend *fines herbes*. This delicate herb, best added after cooking, enhances potato salad, cream cheese, cottage cheese, and freshly sliced tomatoes; spinach, peas, and beans celebrate its touch as well.

Chive. Another member of the fines herbes group, this native of Greece and Italy grows wild in many places, as do other relatives of the onion (actually, lily) family; its name is derived from the Latin "rush leek." In addition to the mild onion flavor of the snipped green stalks, chive offers delicate purple flowers that have been revered for their culinary beauty since they were first mentioned as being present in the gardens of Charlemagne. Try chives in mashed potatoes, green beans, asparagus soup, scrambled eggs and omelets, cream cheese, mayonnaise dressings, soups, salads, and, of course, vichyssoise.

Coriander. A multifaceted flavoring plant, the seeds of this native of North Africa have worked their way into cui-sines of South America, Mexico, China and into *garam masala* of India; the leaves of the herb are called cilantro, fresh coriander, or Chinese parsley. Coriander possesses a strong flavor, reminiscent of lemon and lavender, with a subtle metallic suggestion. Try the ground seeds on roast pork and in pastries, sausages, stuffings, curries, and stews; the leaves impart a true Mexican flavor to sauces, seafood, guacamole, and light cheese dishes.

Dill. Named for the Norse word meaning "to lull," and once used to induce sleep, dill is applied to cuisines as far reaching as Greek, Scandinavian, European, and Slavic. Dill resembles fennel in foliage and offers both seed and leaf for culinary use. Dill is as critical to the Swedish marinated salmon known as gravlax as it is in Russian cookery; in the latter, dill is often married to yogurt or beets. Dill leaf can be used in your kitchen to flavor potato salad, vinegar, shellfish poaching liquids, stuffed eggs, green beans, and sauerkraut; use the seeds for breads, bean soup, steamed artichokes, stews, cucumber dishes, pickles, and sausage.

Fennel. One of the more versatile herbs, fennel produces leafy stalks, seeds, and edible bulbs that are cooked like turnips; of Mediterranean origin, fennel has found its way into the cooking of France, Italy, and the countries of Scandinavia. Fennel seeds are exceedingly strong, yielding one signature flavor of Italian sausages; they also do well in sauerkraut, apple pie, bean soups, shellfish dishes, candies, and beets. Stalks are much milder, finding their ways into preparations of grilled fish, potato salad, spinach, sweet pickles, and soups.

Marjoram. Related to, but milder than, oregano, marjoram is another member of the mint family; its Greek name means "joy of the mountain," a tribute to both its quality and origin. Marjoram is termed the "sausage herb" by German cooks and is touted for the same qualities by the sausage-loving British. Of the available varieties, that labeled "sweet" has the most far-ranging culinary uses. Herb breads, stuffings, and egg dishes benefit from marjoram, as do chowders, beans, meat pies, and roast lamb, duck, and beef. Marjoram can often be used in place of oregano.

Mint. Early Egyptians prized mint for paying tithes and a variety of pharmaceutical and hygienic uses, and probably introduced it to the Romans; it then made its way throughout Europe, where the two culinary varieties, spearmint and peppermint, thrived. Mint is popular in such Middle Eastern dishes as Lebanese *tabbouleh* and has long been regarded for its marriage to roasted lamb. Additional mint magic can be created in apple sauce, stewed pears, and fruit salads; other uses include carrots and peas, cucumbers and yogurt, cream cheese, and pea and bean soups.

Oregano. A member of the mint family, and essential to Greek and Italian cooking, this major herb is also termed "wild marjoram" and "Mexican sage"; of Syrian origin, oregano traveled far and wide, eventually being carted to Mexico by Spanish settlers. Its pungent taste and aroma find their ways into chili dishes, salad dressings, sautéed onions, omelets, zucchini and bean dishes, eggplant, and shrimp salad. A natural with tomatoes, oregano can simply be sprinkled over fresh slices with vinaigrette dressing.

Parsley. Although the ancient Greeks disdained its culinary uses for decorative wreaths, parsley has gained quite a following in contemporary European cookery. A major ingredient in Lebanese tabbouleh, parsley is a constituent of both fines herbes and bouquets garni; it combines with olive oil and garlic to form French *provençale*. Many forms of parsley exist, one of which has become ensconced in Chilean and other South American cookery styles. Soups and salads, stews and casseroles all benefit from a touch of fresh parsley, as will potatoes, rice, mushrooms, meatballs, and dumplings.

Rosemary. A Mediterranean evergreen, rosemary grows along the shore, well within range of the sea's salt spray; "the plant of memory," rosemary is often called the most beautiful and fragrant of all herbs. Taken to England by the Romans, rosemary quickly became an all-European favorite, both in cooking and as a widely used ingredient in medicinal concoctions. In addition to its regal status with roast lamb, rosemary fares well with chicken, pork, stuffings, and dumplings; stews and soups like minestrone really benefit from its presence. Try rosemary with green beans, with orange slices, and in herbal jelly.

Sage. Native to Mediterranean shores, sage was carried by the Romans to England, and from there it traveled to China. In addition to culinary uses, sage was peculiarly steeped and consumed as an age-reducing tea! The strong presence of sage can be toned down with chopped parsley, but its characteristic flavor is welcomed in bread stuffings, sausage, and seafood chowders; cheese sauces and omelets also benefit from careful addition. A natural with pork, sage does wonderful things for veal, game, cream soups, and lima beans.

Savory. A member of the mint family, savory has traveled from native France and Spain to touch the foods of many countries. With a flavor reminiscent of thyme, savory has often been called the "green bean herb," a clear reference to its favorable influence on that vegetable. Savory is available in winter and summer varieties, the latter of which is more highly prized. Try savory in stuffings, meat loaf, chicken dishes, baked onions, asparagus, artichokes, scrambled eggs, cabbage dishes, fish, and peas.

Sorrel. Found predominately in the cooking of England and France, the use of this herb has been recorded since 3000 B.C.; ancient Egyptians and Romans mention its presence in salads. Acidic in flavor, the green leaves must be used sparingly in salads, but can be cooked to great benefit with spinach, cabbage, and beet greens. Sorrel soup is a French classic, and in a sauce, sorrel is served with lamb, beef, and fish; it can also be used in scrambled eggs and omelets.

Tarragon. Another constituent of fines herbes, tarragon lends its aniselike flavor to the classic sauce bearnaise. Native to France and Spain, the dominating flavor of tarragon evidently prompted early users to favor its application to dragon bites! When used with discretion, tarragon complements cream sauces for chicken, veal, and fish and mayonnaise dressings for shrimp; quiches, carrots, omelets, salmon, vinegars, and compound butter are also tarragon candidates.

Thyme. Once used to symbolize strength and bravery, thyme has a strong flavor and must be used with care; many varieties of culinary thyme are found in its native Greece, in French bouquets garni, and throughout European cookery. Combining well with dill and oregano, thyme also marries nicely with brandy, leeks, cream, or wine. Most roasts, meat loaf, and fish dishes can benefit from thyme, as can seafood chowders, other soups, omelets, and various rice dishes; a natural with tomatoes, it also enhances onions, potatoes, and zucchini.

SPICES

Allspice. A berry from a West Indies tree, allspice offers a unique aromatic suggestion of cinnamon, nutmeg, and clove; picked while still green and then dried, it is available whole or ground. The Spanish call this subtly sweet spice *pimento.* Present in Lebanese and Scandinavian cookery, allspice is ideal for marinades and curries, ketchup, and pickles. A touch does wonders for cabbage, potato, and cauliflower soups; puddings, spice cakes, and mincemeat are some dessert uses. Try it in tabbouleh salad, tomato sauce, spinach, and stuffed eggs.

Anise. Thought to be a native of Egypt, this sweetly aromatic seed provides a flavor reminiscent of licorice; it can be found in the cuisines of France, Italy, Mexico, North Africa, South America, and the Middle East. Anise runs the gamut from aperitif to dessert, providing the distinctive flavor of French pernod and Italian sambucca, and it appears in various cookies and breads. A member of the carrot family, anise graces soups, stocks, tomato sauce, baby carrots, halibut steaks, poached pears, and citrus fruits. A variety known as "star anise" is a versatile performer in Chinese cuisine.

Cardamom. An Asian relative of the ginger family, cardamom has found its way into such dishes as Scandinavian pastries and Indian curries. The sweet/sharp flavor of these small seeds blends well with cinnamon and cloves, is reminiscent of ginger, and must be used with discretion. Ground cardamom does well with rice, carrots, melon, and yogurt; try a touch in pancake and waffle batters, as well as in grape jelly. The whole seeds are used to make cordials and also add zest to cups of espresso.

Chili Powder. Not a true spice, this is a blend of flavoring agents whose combination produces the familiar product. Chili pepper, cumin, oregano, garlic powder, and salt are in most blends as might be cloves, allspice, anise, and coriander. A common ingredient in Mexican and Tex-Mex cookery, chili powder can also be used in dips, cocktail spreads, guacamole, barbecued chicken and meat, French dressings, and sausages; combining it with tomato sauce results in an omelet filling.

Cinnamon. Discovered by the Dutch on the island of Ceylon (now Sri Lanka), cinnamon is derived from the bark of a tropical tree; quite mild in its pure form, cinnamon is less piquant than its cousin cassia, which comprises most commercial ground blends. Cinnamon has become a major flavoring in such cuisines as those of Mexico, Greece, Scandinavia, and Africa, to name but a few. Add a touch to chili, moussaka, baklava syrup, mincemeat, and French toast batter. Cinnamon will also sparkle in puddings, breads, sweet potatoes, curries, chocolate items, and fruit desserts; it is a standard in pumpkin pie.

Clove. One of the more aromatic spices, whole cloves are produced by drying the plucked unopened blossom of a bushy tropical tree; native to Madagascar, the Philippines, and Indonesia, the clove is bright red when picked and dark brown when shipped whole or ground. Always removed before service, whole cloves are excellent in marinades, roasted hams, meat stews, pickles, poached fish stock, and sauerbraten. Ground cloves should be carefully tested with fruit compotes and soups, hot drinks, chocolate pudding, beets, and various stuffings for meat and game.

Cumin. Native to Iran and the Mediterranean area, cumin is distributed around the world; it flavors cooking in Europe, Africa, India, South America, the Middle East, and Mexico, where it bears the name *comino*. A relative of the carrot family, cumin provides the aroma and flavor known by anyone who cooks with chili powder; it is also a constituent of curry powder and *garam masala*. If you desire stronger flavor, carefully roast the seeds before grinding them or adding whole to corn soup, guacamole, carrot salad, bean dishes, pepper salad, rice, chicken, potatoes, or any number of fish and shellfish dishes.

Curry Powder. Rather than a single spice, curry powder is a mixture whose distinctive flavor emanates from a blend of such spices as ground clove, chilis, ginger, turmeric, fenugreek, cardamom, and coriander—to name just a few. Associated with Indian cookery, curry powder is an Anglicized version of garam masala, spice blends that are prepared specifically for a particular dish. Strong in character, a touch of curry powder goes a long way with stuffed eggs, crêpe fillings, shellfish dishes, French dressing, rice, stewed pears, lamb entrees, and soups such as chilled Crème Senaglaise.

Fenugreek. This slightly bitter member of the pea family provides the classic aroma one associates with curry powder; a typical ingredient in garam masala mixtures, this seed (either whole or ground) is often used in conjunction with such other blended spices as cumin, fennel, and mustard. While some suggest that a taste of fenugreek reminds them of maple syrup, its more currylike aroma complements potato dishes, soups and stews, okra, lentils and other dried bean dishes, eggplant, and pickled vegetables.

Ginger. The presence of the gnarled root of the ginger plant is strong in Indian and Chinese cuisines, although it has long been one of the most valued spices throughout the culinary world; the perennial favorite gingerbread is thought to have been first baked in Greece in 2800 B.C.! The hot, spicy roots are grated and added to a variety of dishes and are constituents of garam masala. Ginger laces sauerbraten and other pot roasts, is familiar in pumpkin pie and chutney, and can also lend its charms to sweet potatoes, papayas, avocados, and canned fruit; try it in chicken dishes, with fish, and in spice cakes and cookies. When purchasing ginger, look for a smooth, greenish surface; when brown and wrinkled, the roots are woody.

Juniper. This berry from the juniper pine (actually a cypress tree) provides the principal flavor of distilled gin; bittersweet and strong to the taste, dark juniper berries should be counted and crushed before adding to most dishes. When combined with garlic and brandy, juniper is a popular spice in Polish kitchens; also, cooks in the British Isles have long sung its culinary praises. Try juniper in marinades and pâtés, in game dishes, and with lamb, Cornish hens, and braised pork; chicken salad, cabbage, baked beans, and stuffings are more possibilities.

Mace. Harvested as a brilliant red lacy covering from the nutmeg fruit, mace reaches the kitchen from its native Indonesia as a deep, reddish-brown powder; if available whole, the correct name for a piece of mace is blade. Although it is little used in its country of origin, mace interchanges with nutmeg in the cuisines of such countries as Italy, South Africa, Hungary, and England; it is sometimes called the pound cake spice. Mace is used in a variety of desserts that include cherry and chocolate items, preserves, and gingerbread; it also lends interest to carrots, oyster stew, fish sauces, pickles, red cabbage, and beans.

Mustard. One taste of the bright-yellow concoction served in many Chinese restaurants will be sufficient to corroborate the reputation for piquancy of ground mustard; mixed with warm water and allowed to stand for 10 minutes, mustard produces quite a whallop, greatly enhancing slices of British roast beef as well as egg rolls and wontons. Two kinds of unground seeds are available: yellow are mildly flavored and hot; black are more pungent, but also more tame. Try a judicious amount of ground mustard powder in mashed potatoes, cheese and cream sauces, pork chops, and eggs; whole seeds are used in pickling brines and marinades and are tossed in with salad greens.

Nutmeg. Plucked from trees up to 40 feet tall, nutmeg is cloaked with an aril of mace; when removed from its yellow-green shell, the pecan-sized spice is shipped from its native Indonesia. Nutmeg first made its way through India as one of the key spices to reach Europe and one that Columbus sought to discover in his travels. Though he never found this treasured spice, nutmeg ultimately reached the kitchens of the world and is now used in custards, puddings, dough-nuts, and eggnog; nondessert dishes include spinach and cauliflower, cream sauces, cheese dishes, mushrooms, vegetable purées, and cornmeal gnocchi.

Paprika. One of many Capsicum peppers discovered in the New World, paprika has become indelibly associated with Hungarian cookery, although it was initially developed in Turkey; varieties are now raised in Spain and California as well as throughout Eastern Europe. The best paprika is deep to bright red in color; Hungarian is typically piquant, while Spanish is most often sweet. Exceedingly high in vitamin C, paprika finds its way into sausages and marinades and adds flavor to soups and chowders, chicken and shellfish, mayonnaise and sour cream dressings, and dishes that feature pork and veal. Its flavor blends well with caraway and garlic.

Pepper, Black. This is the one that started it all! Once more valued than human life, the small kernel of the *Piper nigrum* family prompted Christopher Columbus and others like him to seek its source and thus control its supply and price. Native to India and to the Indone-sian Spice Islands called the Moluccas, true black pepper is picked while green and spread in the sun to dry. White pepper is the very same berry that is allowed to ripen on the tree; its hull is removed and its core is bleached. Green pepper-corns are merely unripened berries that are immersed in brine (among other preservatives) and sealed. This king of spices has been used to ransom cities and, less aggressively, to stimulate the appetite; its culinary uses run the gamut from lacing an iced aperitif vodka to a dessert of pepper-strewn pears. No vegetable, sauce, soup, or entree—or any other food type—would be inappropriately caressed by a kiss of *Piper nigrum* pepper.

Pepper, Hot and Sweet. When Columbus sailed forth to discover a western route to India, it was for spices—especially pepper—that he searched. When he encountered various plants with pods of green, yellow, and red fruit, and he tasted their piquancy, he mistakenly assumed them to be peppers and named them so. Thus a confusion resulted that has lasted to this day. Dozens of varieties of these Capsicum varieties exist, including such common ones as paprika, cayenne, chilis, and sweet bell. A part of the same organic family that provides tomatoes and tobacco, red pepper returned with Columbus to Europe and from there it circled the globe; the cuisines of China, Africa, Europe, Japan, Korea, India—almost everywhere—share with Mexico and Central and South America the use and appreciation of the red pepper family. From bell pepper sweet to the hell fire of Yucatán *habañeros*, the Capsicum family is a large one indeed. With the expanding popularity and availability of typically Mexican peppers, it is a good idea to become familiar with the piquant properties of some of the more common types. Hot: *jalapeño, serrano, habañeros, chilacas, güero, pasilla, guajillo, chipotle, seco.* Mild: *poblano, ancho, mulato, cascabel.* Care should be taken when handling these often fiery little pods, especially when removing their seeds and veins; always wear gloves and never rub your eyes during or directly after handling.

Saffron. One of the world's most expensive spices, saffron is derived from a tiny Spanish crocus plant; the orange stigmata that each 3-inch plant produces are plucked and then dried to yield their treasure. Saffron contributes a brilliant yellow color and distinctive metallic flavor that are renowned in the cookery of Mediterranean Spain, Italy, and the south of France; Mexican cooks use *achiote* to duplicate the color, though not the flavor, in some of their foods. Saffron is critical to such classics as paella, bouillabaisse, and arroz con pollo. To use, dissolve stigmata "threads" in warm water until the color is obtained.

Sesame Seed. Called Benne seeds along our Atlantic coast, sesame seeds found their way here from western Africa; they are used in the cuisines of China, Korea, Mexico, and the Middle East, in their natural pale color, toasted to a golden brown, or pressed into richly flavored oil. High in fat content, sesame seeds should be watched carefully to prevent burning while toasting. Other than baking applications, sesame seeds are used in salads, candy (halvah), meat loaf, spinach, poultry stuffing, tahini, and many cream pies; in Mexican cookery, they are a key ingredient of the classic *mole poblano.*

Turmeric. The source of the yellow hue in curry powders and prepared mustards, turmeric is sometimes called a "poor man's saffron." Native to India and Jamaica, turmeric is obtained by grinding the root of a plant related to ginger; slightly bitter in taste, it is a key constituent of the Indian spice mixture garam masala. Try conservative amounts of turmeric in curry and rice dishes, chutneys, seafood, chicken, and vegetables.

Three

Appetizers: A Time and A Place

Just as there are no limits to the time of day or meal occasion for the service of buffet appetizers, neither are there limits to their ethnic flavors. In fact, within the fabric of many cuisines there is a special place for appetizers alone, a time when people gather to hone their wits and whet their appetites . . . with savories and socializing around an appetizer buffet. Whether you offer appetizers on a buffet table or in the cocktail lounge, ideas from many countries provide several ways for creative world's fare to grace your menu.

CHINESE DIM SUM

Literally meaning "touch the heart," these Chinese stuffed pastries have been a part of Oriental cuisine since the ages of the Sung Dynasty, more than 300 years before the travels of Marco Polo. Wontons, egg rolls, and "pot stickers" are some of the general categories, and within each is a wealth of Chinese appetizers that can be prepared from fresh or premade wrappings. Wontons can be filled with meat or fish and then steamed or fried. *Siu mai* (small dumplings made in wonton wrappers) contain seasoned ground shrimp and pork; gentle steaming prepares them for the buffet table. Egg rolls, a direct descendant of spring rolls, are filled with shredded meats and vegetables before they are deep fried for ser-

vice. Pot stickers, or *jao tze*, are pork- and shrimp-filled hot water pastry circles that are folded into three-sided pockets and steamed, either with or without a preliminary frying step. Shrimp toasts are a deep-fried item made by spreading bread triangles with a puréed mixture of shellfish and egg whites; *ga li gai goh* are a similar preparation of curried chicken on strips of pie dough. In addition to these dim sum appetizers, Chinese cooks also prepare such "picnic" foods as smoked tea duck, fried chicken wings, barbecued spareribs, tangy stir-fried shrimp, piquant noodle salad, and marinated vegetables; like their Japanese counterparts (see section on Japanese *zensai*), these delights can be served warm or chilled. Most Chinese appetizers are delicious with soy sauce, rice wine vinegar, sweet/sour sauce, or *hoisin* sauce; beer and sake are appropriate beverages.

GREEK MEZES

When the time draws nigh for some *mezethakia*—an assortment of Greek appetizers that combine to form a buffet of vast delights—beverages such as ouzo or roditis help to set a gala food theme. Greek canapés are popular items, spread thickly with caviar, sardines, or anchovy slices; crackers can be used to dip into yogurt spreads or a mixture of eggplant,

olives, and capers. Greek sausage, called *loukania*, is rich with meat, garlic, cinnamon, pepper, and orange peel; herring is smoked and served with olive oil. Little pastries are filled with cheese, spinach, or lamb; mussels are stuffed with rice and herbs; grape leaves burst with lamb, scallions, mint, and dill; cucumbers form "boats" for chopped shrimp, crab, and creamed cheese. Vegetables such as eggplant and zucchini are often frittered and fried; cheese wedges, called *kasseri tigh-anito*, are flamed with brandy and doused with lemon. Samples of souvlakia are appetizer portions of skewered lamb or chicken, served with slices of pepper and onion. If you want to complete the picture with another appropriate wine, complement ouzo and roditis with piney, yellow retsina.

INDONESIAN RIJSTTAFEL

The translation is "rice table," but the practical meaning is lots of good food! This Dutch-Indonesian classic has been toned down dramatically from a pompous history, but still features meats and vegetables in panoramic presentation; accompanied by small bowls of condiment *sambal* and steamed rice, items on a rijsttafel welcome guests to test and sample. Perfect for the stand-up buffet, Indonesian *satés* are skewers of grilled poultry, shrimp, or meat; peanut sauce is a favorite accompaniment. Curried chicken, spiced eggplant wedges, shredded beef and spiced pork, shrimp wafers, fried tofu cubes, spiced hard-boiled eggs, and coconut-flavored fried chicken are just some of the items that could be served in appetizer-sized pieces. Fried banana slices, barbecued ribs, and vegetable curries and dipping sauces can tempt participants in a rijsttafel to cool their palates with a tropical cocktail or iced tea; palm leaves and coconuts provide a touch of atmospheric garnish.

ITALIAN ANTIPASTO

Meaning "before the pasta," these traditional favorites are welcomed at any time and can stand on their own as a buffet drawing card. When raw vegetables or grilled pepper strips need a dipping sauce, *bagna cauda* is the choice; rich with garlic and tangy with anchovies, this is a specialty of the Piedmont area. Chicken livers are ground with prosciutto and spread on toast slices, shrimp are mixed with rice and peppers, mussels are steamed with lemon and parsley or baked with vinegar and garlic, and olives are stuffed with ground meats and cheese for some other regional specialties. All antipasto platters must include slices of flavorful sausages and creamy Italian cheeses, and mushrooms, carrots, and artichoke hearts are marinated in oil and vinegar; melon slices or figs with ham are also common antipasto constituents. The *frittata* is an Italian omelet and often finds its open-faced way onto antipasto presentations; artichokes, spinach, zucchini, and onions are just a few of the possible toppers for wedge-shaped servings. Octopus and squid, fried or marinated in ubiquitous garlic and olive oil, will also be popular. Loaves of crisp bread and carafes of dry white or red wine will complete the scene for an Italian appetizer antipasto buffet.

JAPANESE ZENSAI

Closely related to the Japanese *bento* (picnic box foods), which are items planned to be eaten at room temperature, zensai are tidbits served before a main meal that can be warmed or cool, but always presented with an eye toward garnish and delicate slicing. The variety of shellfish available to Japanese cooks contributes to zensai assortments, as do carrots, cucumber, and daikon, the Japanese white radish. Sushi is a classic Japanese presentation of short-grain rice rolled with raw fish, mushrooms, ginger, or smoked salmon; the mixtures are wrapped in sheets of kelp before being sliced into bite-sized pieces. Sashimi, on the other hand, is a presentation of deftly sliced or cubed raw fish, served with carved vegetables and that piquant Japanese horseradish, *wasabe*. Shrimp also take their place on a zensai table, either breaded and fried or grilled with a sauce. Stuffed mushrooms, broiled oysters, steamed clams in a sweet sauce, chopped duck steamed in sake, marinated asparagus and rounds of cucumbers stuffed with crab meat and vegetables are additional zensai offerings. Sake and beer are traditional beverages, while such dipping sauces as mustard, soy sauce, and horseradish find their places among these delicate foods.

RUSSIAN ZAKUSKI

Although wind and snow may blow across the frigid plains, all's warm when zakuski time draws nigh. This Russian appetizer assortment spreads across both tabletop and culture, and although such an "official" excuse like the Easter celebration poses a definite call for zakuski, virtually any occasion for gathering a group will do. Flavored vodkas and varied loaves of sliced rye breads are almost as profuse as the foods traditionally served, each in its own bowl: marinated vegetables such as radishes, cucumbers, carrots, celery, and beans; caviar of as many sorts as feasible, served with garnishes of onions and sour cream; pickled mushrooms with julienne strips of carrots and celery; smoked salmon; creamed and marinated herring; cheeses and sausages of great diversity; pâtés; oysters, anchovies, sardines, and other seafood; pastries filled with mousses of fish or meat; and vodka, vodka, vodka—icy cold from the freezer or flavored with lemon, pepper, or buffalo grass.

SPANISH TAPAS

The scene shifts to a setting sun over the broad Atlantic, fiery red light flooding the assembled foods. It is time for tapas, the Spanish assortment of individual foods designed to be taken in small doses of large variety, ideally well before a formal meal. Some of the literally dozens of comestibles on a tapas array might include cheeses and fruits; ceviche of fish or scallops—tart with lemon or lime; calamari, fried or in marinade; chorizo and other sausages, grilled with a piquant sauce or simply sliced and offered chilled; pâtés of seafood; pasta salads; fried squid stuffed with seasoned pork; sautéed frog legs, shining with a deep red tomato sauce; skewers of lamb or shrimp, with a drape of olive oil, garlic, and paprika. An occasion in its own right, a tapas theme might be enhanced by guitar and flamenco, pitchers of fruity sangria, or slightly chilled glasses of hearty dry sherry. Regardless of the beverage, the list of foods, as well as the reasons to serve them, go on and on.

TURKISH RAKI TABLE

Often refered to as "lion's milk," Turkish raki is a brandy-type beverage flavored with anise; similar to both Greek ouzo and French pastis, raki turns cloudy when diluted with water. Diluted to the taste, or taken straight from the bottle, raki has spawned the raki table, a Turkish social institution focused on the beverage and an array of cocktail appetizers. Often extending into the wee hours, a raki table offers Americans a taste of another cultural buffet event. Cold dishes include feta cheese and olives of many descriptions, sliced tomatoes and cucumbers with a dipping sauce of cheese and herbs, sardines, and marinated native bonito. Snow almonds, in a unique method for serving these nuts, are first soaked in water, then rubbed and drained, and presented in a bowl filled with ice. Warm selections on the raki table might include cheese or meat-filled boereks, little packages of phyllo dough that are baked to a golden brown; hanim parmaği are little fingers of deep-fried spiced ground beef; yalanci dolma are the Turkish version of miniature stuffed grape leaves; fried mussels are served in a variety of ways, including with a tarator dipping sauce of pine nuts and garlic. Rosé wine or chilled beer make suitable alternatives to the "lion's milk" if a more subdued "roar" is desired.

Baked Clams

INGREDIENTS	TEST QUANTITY: 8	SERVICE QUANTITY: 50	METHOD
Littleneck clams, shucked and chopped	2 doz.	12 doz.	Distribute chopped clams in open shell halves.
Butter, melted, unsalted	1 cup	3 lb.	Combine and divide among shells.
Almonds, chopped	$\frac{1}{4}$ cup	$1\frac{1}{2}$ cups	
Tomato, medium, peeled, seeded, chopped	2	4 lb.	
Green pepper, minced	$\frac{1}{4}$ cup	$1\frac{1}{2}$ cups	
Garlic, minced	5 cloves	3 tbsp.	
Shallots, minced	$\frac{1}{4}$ cup	$1\frac{1}{2}$ cups	
Parsley, chopped	$\frac{1}{2}$ cup	3 cups	
White wine, dry	$\frac{1}{4}$ cup	$1\frac{1}{2}$ cups	
Bread crumbs, very dry, sifted	$\frac{3}{4}$ cup	1 lb.	
Salt	to taste	to taste	
Pepper, black, freshly ground	to taste	to taste	
Paprika	to taste	to taste	
Bread crumbs	$\frac{3}{4}$ cup	1 lb.	Sprinkle over.
Parmesan cheese, grated	$\frac{1}{4}$ cup	$1\frac{1}{2}$ cups	
Butter, melted	$\frac{1}{2}$ cup	$1\frac{1}{2}$ lbs.	Sprinkle over. Bake at 350°F until golden, about 10 minutes.

SPECIAL HANDLING FOR BUFFET SERVICE: *Serve these northeast American favorites from a heated tray or shallow insert pan set over dual heating units. Keep covered to maintain optimum heat level. If desired, substitute chopped fresh spinach for the parsley, and add grated Parmesan cheese to the bread crumbs.*